WH
WEIRDEST THING ABOUT ANIMALS?

BLOOMSBURY
CHILDREN'S BOOKS
LONDON OXFORD NEW YORK NEW DELHI SYDNEY

To Mary and Alice, a couple of cheeky monkeys who are also the cat's pyjamas. - E.B-H

To my ever-so-curious son, Ethan. - J.T

BLOOMSBURY CHILDREN'S BOOKS
Bloomsbury Publishing Plc
50 Bedford Square, London WC1B 3DP, UK
Bloomsbury Publishing Ireland Limited
29 Earlsfort Terrace, Dublin 2, D02 AY28, Ireland

First published in Great Britain in 2026 by Bloomsbury Publishing Plc

A catalogue record for this book is available from the British Library

ISBN: PB: 978-1-5266-8515-5
eBook: 978-1-5266-8978-8; Audio: 978-1-0372-0853-9
2 4 6 8 10 9 7 5 3 1
Printed and bound in Great Britain by Clays Ltd, Elcograf S.p.A

MIX
Paper | Supporting responsible forestry
FSC® C018072
FSC www.fsc.org

To find out more about our authors and books visit www.bloomsbury.com and sign up for our newsletters

For product safety related questions contact productsafety@bloomsbury.com

EDWARD BROOKE-HITCHING

WHAT'S THE WEIRDEST THING ABOUT ANIMALS?

Illustrated by
JEZ TUYA

BLOOMSBURY
CHILDREN'S BOOKS
LONDON OXFORD NEW YORK NEW DELHI SYDNEY

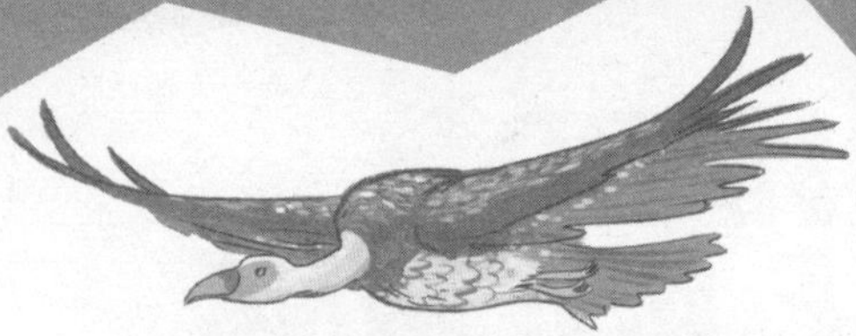

CONTENTS

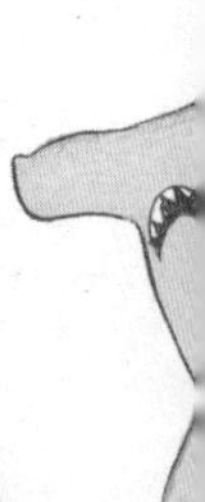

INTRODUCTION

On every continent, in every country, in every garden, there are billions of peculiar creatures living alongside us. Many of them have been on this planet long before humans even existed. Most of them are also living in secret – scientists are discovering thousands of new animals every day, and we know that there are still millions more out there to find.

In fact, every species has something fascinating and bizarre about it – whether it's **worms that glow red and green like a traffic light** (see p.97), **fish that live in trees** (see p.113) or **birds with claws bigger than those of a grizzly bear** (see p.136). Basically, the animal world is massively, wonderfully weird. But have you ever wondered just *how* weird things get?

What's the weirdest thing about turtles, for example? Is it that some can breathe through their bottoms? How about piranhas? Did you know that they can bark like a dog? Or that butterflies have ears on their wings? That wasps can make paper? That wombat poop is cube-shaped? This book is full of answers to all the truly important questions like these, that you (quite sensibly) never thought to ask. Are you curious about why the world's grumpiest frog is so sticky? (See p.189.) What's so interesting about the boring clam? (See p.74.) How do you make a turkey blush? (See p.148.) And where's the best place to see a weasel war dance? (See p.36.)

So hang on to your explorer's helmet, slap on some sunscreen and get ready for ridiculousness, because we're about to go on the world's weirdest safari ...

HOW TO TALK TO ANIMALS AROUND THE WORLD

In English, we say that **bees** *buzz*. But elsewhere in the world, they say bees *taneen* (Arabic), *ngung-ngung* (Batak), *gun-gun* (Bengali), *wēng wēng* (Mandarin Chinese), *sum* (Danish), *bhun bhun* (Nepali) and *zum zum* (Portuguese).

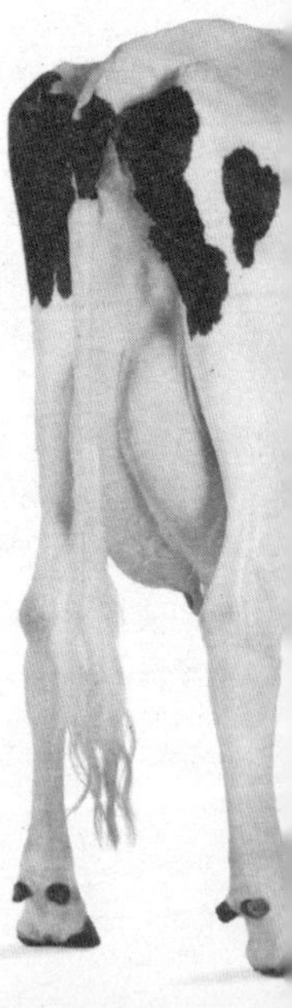

CHOO CHOO!

Birds *tweet*, but they also *ciu-ciu* (Albanian), *piu piu* (Catalan), *ji ji zha zha* (Mandarin Chinese), *piep piep* (German), *choo choo* (Serbian), *kvitter kvitter* (Swedish) and *koo koo* (Tamil).

Roosters *cock-a-doodle-do*, but they also *tsoo-ghoo-roo-ghoo* (Armenian), *kukuriku* (Croatian), *kykkeliky* (Danish), *chicchirichi* (Italian), *kukhuri kaa* (Nepali) and *oooooo* (Vietnamese).

CHICCHIRICHI!

BUU!

Cows *moo*, but they also *ngoah* (Arabic), *hamba* (Bengali), *buu* (Czech), *muh* (Danish), *boe* (Dutch), *eum-mae* (Korean), *ungaa* (Tagalog, Philippines) and *um-bo* (Vietnamese).

Dogs *woof*, but they also *ham-ham* (Albanian), *haf-haf* (Czech), *ouah ouah* (French), *wau-wau* (German), *voff-voff* (Icelandic), *hav-hav* (Turkish) and *gau-gau* (Vietnamese).

Frogs *ribbit*, but they also *kwaak* (Afrikaans), *krooks krooks* (Estonian), *tarr tarr* (Hindi) and *vrak vrak* (Turkish). **Bonus fact:** the Ancient Greeks said frogs make this noise: *brekekekex koax koax*.

Horses *neigh*, but they also *iihihihi* (Albanian), *saheel* (Arabic), *ii-haha* (Czech), *vrinsk* (Danish), *wiehiehie* (German), *yihaa* (Indonesian), *iii-haaa* (Polish) and *gnägg* (Swedish).

Pigs *oink-oink*, but they also *hunk-hunk* (Albanian), *ghnot ghnot* (Bengali), *rok-rok* (Croatian), *groin groin* (French), *grok grok* (Indonesian), *puhi-puhi* (Japanese) and *noff noff* (Danish).

Sheep *baa*, but they also *mee* (Basque), *mæh* (Danish), *meh* (Dutch), *beeh* (French), *mah* (German), *bee* (Hungarian), *mbek* (Indonesian) and *bae-bae* (Thai).

A GROUP OF WHAT IS CALLED A WHAT?!

A **congregation** of alligators

A **shrewdness** of apes

A **cauldron** of bats

A **sleuth** of bears

A **gang** of buffalo

A **kaleidoscope** of butterflies

A **caravan** of camels

An **army** of caterpillars

A **clowder** of cats

A **quiver** of cobras

A **murder** of crows

A **pace** of donkeys

A **bed** of eels

A **parade** of elephants

A **business** of ferrets

A **flamboyance** of flamingos

A **skulk** of foxes

An **army** of frogs

A **tower** of giraffes

A **herd** of guinea pigs

A **bloat** of hippopotamuses

A **cackle** of hyenas

A **shadow** of jaguars

A **smack** of jellyfish

A **mob** of kangaroos

A **loveliness** of ladybirds

A **conspiracy** of lemurs

A **leap** of leopards

A **barrel** of monkeys

A **romp** of otters

A **pandemonium** of parrots

A **prickle** of porcupines

An **unkindness** of ravens

A **crash** of rhinoceroses

A **building** of rooks

A **maelstrom** of salamanders

A **scurry** of squirrels

A **wedge** of swans

An **ambush** of tigers

A **venue** of vultures

A **wisdom** of wombats

A **zeal** of zebras

MARVELLOUSLY
MAGNIFICENT
MAMMALS

Mammals are running, climbing, jumping, hopping, swinging, swimming – some even flying – in every continent and in every ocean in the world. They're vertebrates (meaning they have a spine), they have hair or fur, the females feed milk to their young, and they're warm-blooded. You might have noticed this includes you and your family, though hopefully not too much of the 'fur' part. You've probably already met enough humans to know how weird we are – but what about some of our odder animal cousins we share this category with? How weird do *they* get? Let's meet the family ...

Anteaters

Giant anteaters are about the same size as a German shepherd dog, but their brains are only slightly bigger than a pea.

The giant anteater keeps its front claws sharp by tucking them into its palms and walking on its knuckles. This doesn't slow it down though – in a hurry, it can reach speeds of

30 miles per hour (mph)! It also has no teeth, but has a tongue that's 61 centimetres (cm) long, to scoop food into its mouth.

The French artist Salvador Dalí had a pet anteater that he would take for walks around Paris on a lead in the 1960s.

Apes And Other Primates

Apes have fingerprints very similar to humans. In 1975, English police went to the Ape House at London Zoo and at Twycross Zoo in Leicestershire to take the fingerprints of **chimpanzees** and **orangutans** to make sure they weren't responsible for any unsolved crimes.

The name 'Gorilla' goes back over 2,000 years to the year 480 BCE, when the ancient North-African explorer Hanno the Navigator described a tribe that he met. He called them *Gorillai*, which means 'hairy women'.

Gorillas talk with their **STINK**. While humans spend a lot of time and money on trying to smell nicer, gorillas use their stinky body odour to communicate with each other. Silverbacks (older males) can 'announce' to a group that they've arrived by letting off a powerful smell, and if they need to hide from strangers, they can shut it off. (Scientists discovered this by following, and sniffing, the same male gorilla for months.)

A female gorilla named Koko was taught sign language. She was remarkably clever – she had a vocabulary of over 1,000 signs (she called herself 'Queen'), and understood over 2,000 words of spoken English. She even had her own pet kitten after asking for one for Christmas.

Gibbons that are in love like to sing duets with their partner.

Baby lemurs are born with their eyes wide open,

ready to go. For food, they almost entirely eat papyrus reeds, the same plants that the ancient Egyptians used to make paper.

There's also the **white-footed sportive lemurs**. They like to keep to themselves and avoid everyone, including their own family. They communicate with each other by sharing the same toilet and leaving pee and poo as messages for their relatives.

A new kind of monkey was recently discovered in Asia with a very small, upside-down nose. Scientists have nicknamed him 'Snubby'. When it rains, the water can fall straight down the nose of these monkeys, making them sneeze. They normally spend rainy days covering their faces with their arms to stop the water falling into their nose or tucking their heads between their legs until the rain stops.

Monkeys like to wash themselves in their own **PEE** in the same way humans use perfume. It makes them smell better to their mates.

Male proboscis monkeys with the biggest noses attract the most females.

Mandrills of the African rainforests are the world's largest monkeys and have beautiful colours: blue and red faces, olive-green fur and bright blue and red bottoms. Scientists have seen them make toothpicks from twigs, which they also use to clean their ears and pick at their toenails.

Marmosets of South America are tiny monkeys (they can fit in your hand) and are the only primates other than humans that don't mind if you stare into their eyes – most other primates will think you're trying to pick a fight with them and they'll get angry.

The **pygmy marmoset** is the world's smallest monkey. It weighs about the same as a cricket ball.

Orangutans live on only two islands: Borneo and Sumatra in Southeast Asia. They look bright orange when the Sun catches their hair, but when they move into the shade, they seem to change to a

shadowy colour. Their dark skin lets them hide in the gloom like ninjas. The word 'orangutan' comes from the Malay words *orang* and *hutan*, and means 'person of the forest'.

Recently, some orangutans in a Dutch zoo forgot how to swing from trees, and so zookeepers brought in a human Olympic gymnast to show them how to do it.

In 2017, the zookeepers at Apenheul Primate Park in Apeldoorn, the Netherlands, made an app for their orangutans to help them find love. The female orangutans can swipe through pictures of males to see if there's one they want to have a baby with. (The keepers had to make a strong steel case for the iPad to protect it from the orangutans' excited tapping, but even this was destroyed by one female ape nicknamed by her keepers 'Demolition Woman'.)

As they fall asleep, orangutans blow raspberries at each other.

Armadillos

The Aztec name for armadillo translates to 'turtle rabbit'.

The **screaming hairy armadillo** of central and southern parts of South America is exactly what it sounds like. The smallest of all the hairy armadillos, at 22 to 40 cm in length, it has a tendency to loudly sob, squeal and scream if threatened.

3.2 million years ago, there was a giant armadillo called a *Glyptodon* that lived in South America. It was the size of a car, with a shell so big that a human could use an empty one as a house.

Badgers

Badgers can create huge networks of tunnels for their homes, which are called setts. One badger sett in the UK was found to have 12 entrances and more than 300 metres of tunnels, which is about the length of three football pitches. To build this, the badgers must have moved 25 tonnes of soil – and all without mechanical diggers!

In 1903, US President Theodore Roosevelt had a pet badger in the White House. His daughter wrote that Josiah the Badger 'is always amusing us with his antics, like shredding the furniture with his sharp little claws, or chasing the gardener up a tree. Father just throws his head back and laughs his booming laugh.'

A badger's sense of smell is 800 times more powerful than ours.

The leader of a group of badgers marks every member by 'bum pressing'. It rubs its backside against the other badgers to mark them with its scent. This means that if an intruder makes it into their sett, the badgers can tell instantly if it doesn't belong.

Bats

Bats can fly as high as eagles! The **Mexican free-tailed bat** is the fastest mammal on Earth, able to hit the stupendous speed of 100 mph. This bat also holds another record, for being the highest-flying bat. They've been recorded flying over 3,000 metres up – the same height that eagles like to cruise at. Bats can swim, and some can even run along the ground – vampire bats have been seen chasing their prey on foot.

Vampire bats look after each other – if one is ill and can't go out to find food, its friend will suck extra blood from animals and then return home and VOMIT the blood all over the sickly bat as a gift.

Bats come in wildly different sizes: in Thailand, the **Kitti's hog-nosed bat** (also called the bumblebee bat) weighs less than a penny and is the world's smallest mammal. **West African woolly bats** are so small and light that they live in the webs of spiders.

'Flying fox' bats, on the other hand, which are found in parts of Australia, India and Southeast Asia, can be enormous, with wingspans of up to 1.8 metres. On hot days, they make their own

air conditioning – they hang upside down and use their giant wings to fan themselves cool.

Bears

Adult bears can run at a speed of 40 mph, which is as fast as a greyhound.
They also have bites so powerful that they could **CRUSH** a bowling ball in their jaws.

What should you do if you meet a bear in the wild? Well, if you're attacked by a brown bear you should play dead, but if you do this with a *black bear*, you'll be dead for real. Some people also advise that with black bears, you should take off all your clothes and slowly walk away. So, it's probably best just to avoid bears altogether?

Here's a weird fact: all **polar bears** are Irish. They may live in the Arctic today, but all polar bears are descended from brown bears that lived in Ireland over 10,000 years ago.

Most polar bears are born twins.

Polar bears are black – they have jet-black skin hidden under thick fur that isn't actually white, but transparent. It looks white because it's reflecting light. Polar bears are also the only mammal with hair on the soles of their feet, which helps them to stay warm.

In 1235, King Henry III of England was given a polar bear by the King of Norway. It lived at the Tower of London, where it was given a long leash so it could swim out and catch fish in the River Thames.

The first living thing to test an ejector seat in a US Air Force jet was a two-year-old black bear named Yogi, who was ejected from the plane over 10,000 metres up in the air on 21 March 1962. Yogi landed by parachute 7 minutes and 49 seconds later, a little dazed but unharmed.

Only four animals have blue tongues: the black bear, the chow chow dog, the giraffe and the blue-tongued skink lizard.

Camels

Baby camels don't have humps.

Saudi Arabia has camel beauty contests. 30,000 of the prettiest camels compete for a prize total of $32 million and the title of 'Miss Camel'. A beautiful camel must have a bright coat of hair, an elegant neck and a shapely hump. In 2018, 12 camels were disqualified from a beauty contest in Saudi Arabia when it was found that their owners had cheated by artificially making their animals have poutier lips.

Camels have three pairs of eyelids and can seal their nostrils shut to keep in water vapour, and keep out any sand blowing around.

Camel pee is as thick as syrup. This is because their kidneys and intestines are so good at absorbing water they drink that very little is left to pee out.

If you annoy a camel, make sure you're wearing a raincoat. They can spit on you if they're irritated, and you're unlikely to get away in time because they can spit a long way. The furthest recorded camel spit-missile is 36.8 metres!

Cats

Cats don't just have whiskers on their faces, but also on the backs of their legs. Whiskers help cats sense movement and changes in their surroundings, like a kind of 'cat radar'.

If a human jumped into your lap and headbutted you, it would be a bit insulting. But when cats headbutt you, it's actually a sign of affection, like a human high-five. They're also doing it to rub pheromones on you to claim you as their property. Like a human fingerprint, a cat's noseprint is unique.

Almost all tortoiseshell-coloured cats are female. Only about 1 in 3,000 tortoiseshell cats are boys.

In 2004, a man named Jake Perry had a Guinness World Record for owning the world's oldest cat. The next year he won the record again with a **DIFFERENT CAT**. So what does he do to give his moggies such a long life? The secret, he says, is feeding them a breakfast of bacon, eggs, asparagus and coffee every morning.

Julius Caesar, King Henry II, King Charles XI and Napoleon Bonaparte were all terrified of cats.

Cheetahs

Cheetahs can reach a speed of 112 km/h (kilometres per hour) in just three seconds, which is more powerful than most Ferrari sports cars.

Cheetahs are so shy that zoos sometimes give them support dogs as companions to make them more comfortable.

Cows

Cows only have a full set of bottom teeth – they don't need upper teeth for eating grass. So they can't technically bite you, but beware, they might 'gum' you. Cows pick up grass by curling their tongues round it. It dissolves slightly in their stomachs (cows have one stomach, with four chambers), then they cough it back up, chew it and swallow it again.

It's so cold in Siberia, where temperatures can drop to –55 degrees Celsius, that many Russian farmers give their cows fur bras to wear, to stop their udders from freezing.

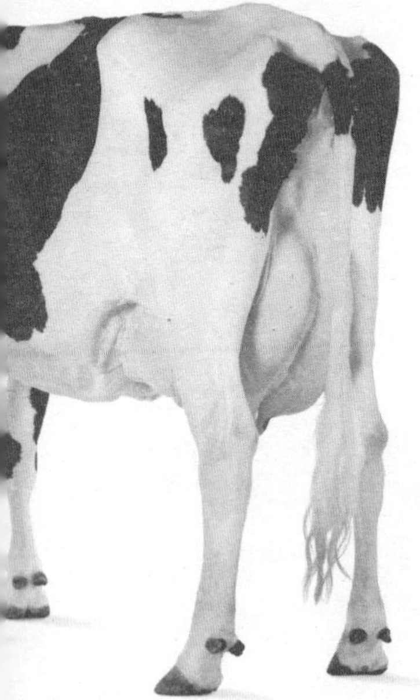

'Cow blowing' is practised in many countries around the world to increase the amount of milk a cow will produce. It's very simple: you walk around to the back of a cow, lift its tail and **BLOW** into its bottom.

Cows have an amazing sense of smell – they can detect a scent from six miles away. They can also climb stairs, but they can't go down them!

Deer

The **leaf muntjac**, or leaf deer, is a tiny species of deer found in Myanmar, Southeast Asia. It was given its name by local hunters, who found it was so small that they could wrap up the whole animal in one large plant leaf. It's about 50 cm tall (about the same size as a beagle), with antlers 2 cm high.

Deer don't just eat grass – some have been seen eating birds, mice and reptiles.

Deer see the colour blue particularly well – in fact, they see blue objects about 20–25 times better than humans.

In 2018, a train in Japan was fitted with powerful outside speakers so the train can make loud snorts and bark like a dog to scare deer out of its way.

Dogs

King Henry III of France (1551–1589) liked to carry around six puppies in a basket around his neck. According to legend, the dogs barked at people he didn't trust.

Miniature Pekingese dogs are also called 'Sleeve Pekingese'. This comes from an old Chinese custom of making the dogs as small as possible so that they could be kept in the sleeves of members of the royal household. This was especially useful for self-defence – the dogs would leap out of the sleeves and chase away attackers.

Dogs have a powerful sense of smell. For example, they can smell what time of day it is, and what happened in a room two hours before. Dogs can also smell whale poo from a mile away. Scientists on Canada's Vancouver Island use a team of 17 dogs to hunt for poo samples of whales, owls and other animals to study.

There has only ever been one dog to serve in the British Royal Navy, a Great Dane named Able Seaman Just Nuisance, who was a British sailor in South Africa between 1939 and 1944. He

was given the surname 'Nuisance' because of his habit of sleeping in small corridors, where people would trip over him.

Dolphins

What do dolphins drink? In fact, adult dolphins don't drink anything, they get their fluids from eating the fish they catch. Even baby dolphins don't exactly 'drink' their mum's milk – dolphin milk is as thick as toothpaste, as it's almost **50 per cent FAT** (cow milk is only 4 per cent fat).

To help them glide smoothly through the water, dolphins shed their skin constantly in flakes, like dandruff. It takes just two hours for them to shed their entire outer layer.

The Amazon river dolphin of South America is also called the **pink dolphin**. During the rainy seasons, the Amazon and Orinoco rivers flood across thousands of miles of rainforest – this is when you might catch the unusual sight of a pink dolphin swimming through a forest, enjoying its newly expanded habitat. While we don't know for certain what makes them turn pink, we know that pink dolphins turn even pinker when they're excited or surprised, like humans when we blush.

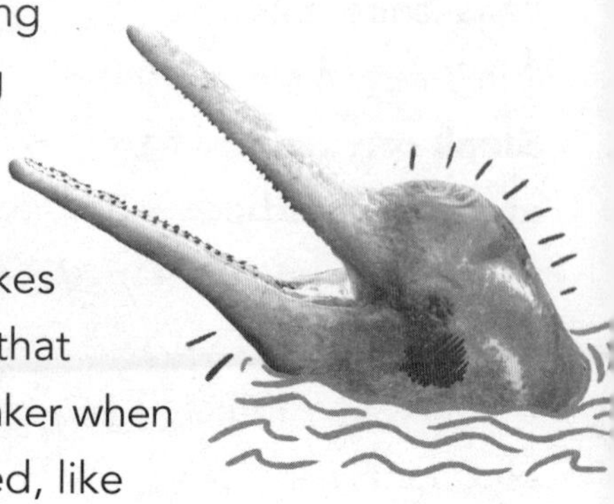

To get the attention of females, humpback dolphins balance sponges on their noses.

Dolphins are as intelligent as apes. A dolphin named Kelly was trained by scientists in Mississippi, USA, to pick up rubbish in her tank. For every piece she collected, she was given a treat. Kelly loved treats, and she was clever, so she crafted a plan. She picked up a large piece of paper and hid it under a rock. She then tore off little bits and brought each one to her trainer to get separate treats.

Elephants

Baby elephants suck their trunks for comfort, just like how human children suck their thumbs.

Elephants and humans are the only animals that have chins.

Elephants aren't frightened of mice, but they are scared of bees – Kenyan farmers surround their fields with beehives to keep elephants out. People in Tanzania keep elephants away by throwing balloons filled with chilli powder at them – elephants hate spicy things.

No one has ever seen an elephant jump.

African elephants can use their feet to 'hear'. Vibrations from the ground go up their front legs and shoulder bones, and into their middle ear.

If you're desperate for a drink and you're near an elephant, you can squeeze a few drops of water out of elephant poo. (But only if you're really desperate.)

Ferrets

The word 'ferret' comes from the Latin *furittus,* which means 'little thief'. When they're happy, ferrets perform the 'weasel war dance', which involves a lot of hopping around and bumping into things. Weasels use the same routine to hypnotise smaller animals that they're trying to catch.

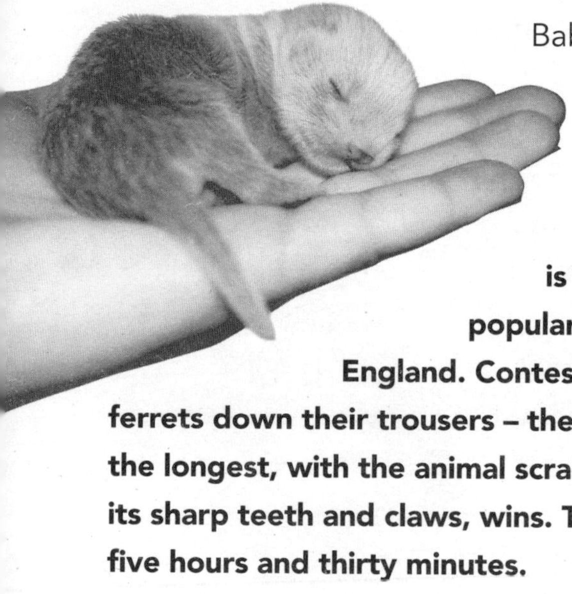

Baby ferrets are so small that they can fit on a teaspoon.

'Ferret-legging' is a sport that was popular in Yorkshire, England. Contestants put live ferrets down their trousers – the person who lasts the longest, with the animal scrabbling around with its sharp teeth and claws, wins. The world record is five hours and thirty minutes.

Ferret-racing is another sport that involves ferrets sprinting down their own tube. It's very unpredictable, as sometimes the animals stop and fall asleep in the middle of the race.

Foxes

Iceland's only native animal is the Arctic fox.

Foxes in Australia have been seen climbing trees to hunt **koalas**.

In the Patagonian region of South America, foxes were kept as pets 1,500 years ago before domestic dogs arrived.

Gazelles

Gazelles HONK when they see something worrying.

The **dorcas gazelle**, which wanders the northern African deserts, doesn't pee. To avoid dehydrating in the heat, it lets out all its waste in solid pellets.

Sand gazelles also have a trick for surviving the heat: in an emergency they can SHRINK their heart, liver and other organs that need a lot of oxygen. This means that they breathe less, and lose less water when exhaling.

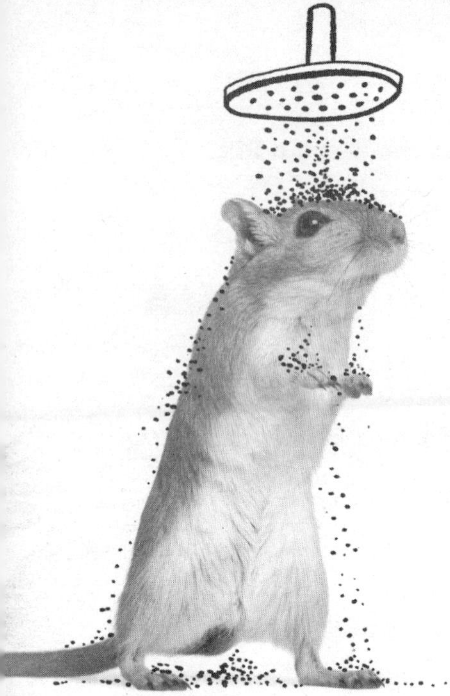

Gerbils

Scientists have counted over 100 different species of gerbils. These include real species names like **Cheesman's gerbil**, the **South African hairy-footed gerbil** and the **pleasant gerbil**.

Gerbils wash themselves with sand, not water.

If you catch a gerbil by its tail, it can shed it to escape you.

Giraffes

Giraffes are the only vertebrates that don't yawn; and although we used to think their necks were too long for them to make much noise, at night they actually hum a deep, musical song, even though they don't have vocal cords.

Giraffes use their long necks to spot predators approaching, but also to fight with each other.

When a male wants to show he's the strongest, he'll wallop another male with his neck and head.

Giraffes are incredibly STINKY – if you were downwind of one, you could smell it from 244 metres away. The smell is used to attract other giraffes, but also to repel bugs and parasites.

A baby giraffe is born wearing 'angel slippers' on its feet, which are smooth coatings that it sheds a few days after it's born. This also helps protect the mother from the baby's sharp hooves.

Goats

The first female to circumnavigate the globe was a milk-goat, who travelled with Captain James Cook (1728–1779) and provided milk to the sailors on board his ship HMS *Endeavour* on a voyage around the world between 1768–1771. When they returned to England, 'The Well-Travelled Goat' became a celebrity.

The pupil of a goat's eye is rectangular, unlike ours which are circular. This means the goat has extra wide vision to help it look out for predators. Goats sneeze to warn each other of danger.

Mountain goats aren't goats, they're actually a kind of antelope.

Hamsters

Hamsters can change colour in the wild. The grey-brown coat of the **winter white dwarf hamster** turns white in winter. This acts like camouflage in the snow. Hamsters love running on their exercise wheels so much that some can run 9 kilometres (km) in one night.

Hamsters have been hiding food for a long time. In 2003, German scientists discovered a burrow hiding 1,800 fossilised nuts. They were probably stashed there by a large hamster 17 million years ago.

Hedgehogs

The ancient Roman writer Pliny the Elder claimed that hedgehogs like to climb trees, punch apples off the branches, roll over on them and then run off with the fruit caught in their spiky spines. While this isn't true, hedgehogs have been known to climb up walls and enter open first-floor windows.

Hedgehogs use the same muscle to roll into a ball as they use to frown – which means if you see a rolled-up hedgehog, it's also frowning at its head and its bottom.

Hippopotamuses

Hippopotamuses can't actually swim. When they're underwater, they're walking on the riverbed.

'Hippopotamus' comes from the ancient Greek word *hippopótamos,* which means 'river horse'. Sometimes, the hippopotamus will spin its tail like a windmill while it's pooping. This helps to SPRAY ITS POO around to mark its territory.

Horses

Horses have more facial expressions than **chimpanzees**.

When vacuum cleaners were first invented, they were so big and heavy that they had to be pulled by horse.

If you want to work out whether a horse is right-hooved or left-hooved, look at its hair. If it's growing counter-clockwise, there's a 75 per cent chance that they prefer their left hoof.

Kangaroos

Before they were hunted to extinction, there used to be kangaroos that were 2.74 metres tall, which is taller than the tallest human to ever live.

Joeys (baby kangaroos) are born without back legs – they grow them in their mother's pouch. When the first European explorers to reach Australia saw kangaroos, they saw the joeys in the pouches and assumed that the kangaroo had two heads.

Male kangaroos pose like bodybuilders to show off their muscles to females.

Koala Bears

***Koala* is an Australian Aboriginal word meaning 'no drink'. Koalas rarely drink water, as they get their moisture from eating eucalyptus leaves (which, by the way, are poisonous to most animals except the koala).**

Koala bears are technically **NOT** bears. They're marsupials, a separate class of mammal that carry their young in their pouches, and so are more closely related to kangaroos than true bears.

Koala mums can do something amazing (but rather disgusting) – they can make a mushy food for their babies, called pap. It's made from their POO. This helps the baby learn to eat solid food, before they can eat eucalyptus leaves like their mum.

Lions

Lions have spots! Or more accurately, they have them when they're young. Their yellow coats have patterns of rosettes and dots which gradually fade away as they get older.

In the 1960s in London, you could buy baby leopards, lions, alligators and elephants at Harrods.

Not all male lions have manes. In the hottest parts of Africa, like the Tsavo National Park in Kenya, male lions are 'maneless'. This is probably because the temperature is too high for the extra hair – imagine wearing a thick wool scarf on a hot summer's day!

Llamas

It's illegal to ride a llama in the UK, for their sake – it's bad for their backs.

When a llama is annoyed with another llama, it sticks its tongue out at it.

The Inca people of Peru would make fires with piles of dry llama poo to stay warm.

Meerkats

Meerkats are immune to the poisons of some venomous snakes, just like their cousin, the **mongoose**.

When the meerkat attacks a scorpion, it doesn't give it a chance to use its venomous sting – the meerkat snatches it and BITES OFF its stinger. It then rubs the scorpion on the ground to get rid of any venom on its skin before it eats it. Clever!

Meerkats have incredible vision. The black patches around their eyes cut down the Sun's glare, and they can spot birds from miles away. Their long, horizontal pupils allow them to have widescreen vision without turning their heads.

Zookeepers have stopped meerkats from fighting each other by rubbing Vicks VapoRub on the animals, which prevents them from being able to smell each other.

Mice

Mice can squeeze through a hole as small as 6 millimetres (mm) wide.

Mice don't mind the smell of human women, but they hate the stink of human men.

Male mice attract female mice by singing love songs at a pitch too high for us to hear.

Mice poop a lot. They leave about 36,000 droppings every year.

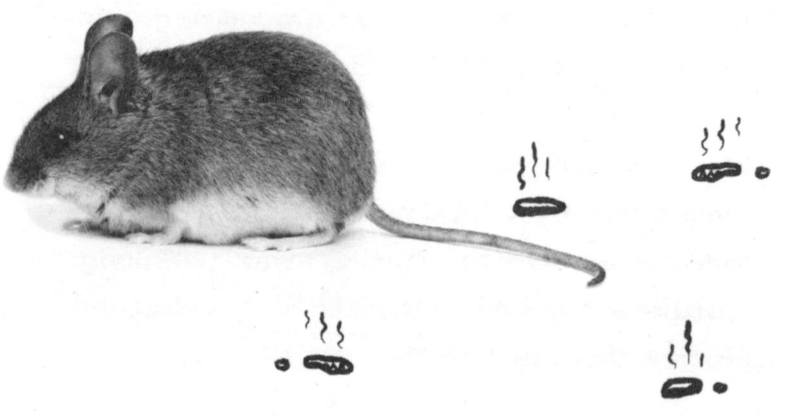

Moles

The golden mole is more closely related to otter shrews than other kinds of moles. Its organs are so good at using as little water as possible that the golden mole never needs to drink water for its entire life.

There are no moles in Ireland. They've never been ableto cross over from the UK mainland.

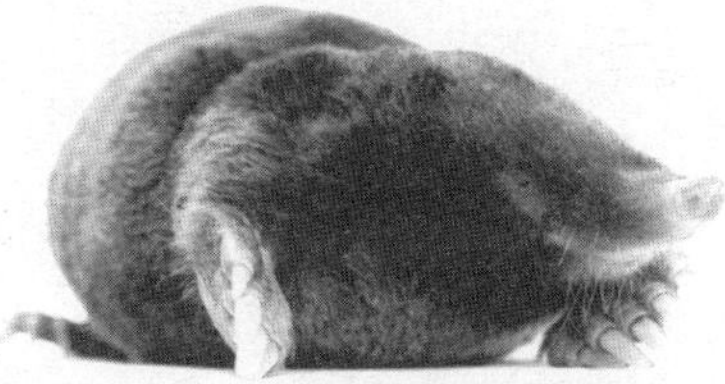

Moles mainly feed on earthworms – they paralyse them with their TOXIC SALIVA, and carry them back to a larder where they store them to eat a worm-dinner later.

Otters

Sea otters have a secret pocket of loose skin under their arms that they like to keep stones in – they use the pebbles to smash open food such as clams.

Sea otters have the THICKEST fur of any animal. Their fur is so thick that the cold water they swim in doesn't ever reach their skin. They can have as many as a million hairs per square inch – on average humans have fewer than 100,000 on our whole head.

When they lie floating on the water, otters hold hands so they don't drift away from each other.

If you sniff fresh otter poo, you'll notice it smells just like jasmine tea.

Pandas

Pandas can mark out their territory by doing a handstand up against a tree, and then **PEEING** as high as they can.

A panda's paw has six digits – five fingers, and an extra 'fake thumb' which is really a large part of their wrist bone, which they use to help grip bamboo while eating.

Even though you only really see pandas eating bamboo, they are actually carnivores – their digestive systems are able to process meat, but they gave up eating meat millions of years ago (probably because other animals were too hard to catch). But even today, if they catch a **rat**, pandas will eat it.

You can make paper from dried panda poop. Pandas poo an average of 10 kilograms (kg) of waste, which is heavier than the heaviest bowling ball.

Pangolins

Pangolins, also known as 'scaly anteaters' (although they're not related to anteaters), don't have any teeth. Instead, they swallow small rocks with their food to grind it up in their stomach.

A pangolin's tongue is longer than its body.

Pangolins don't want any distractions when they eat, so they close up their ears and nostrils to focus on the meal.

Pigs

Pigs can't look up at the sky, so they never see the stars.

Until it went extinct, there was a breed of pig called the **Lincolnshire Curly Coat**, which had a long woolly white coat just like a sheep.

Every morning at the Kitagawa pig farm in Japan, the pigs are treated with a drink of green tea to help them relax.

Duck-billed Platypuses

Duck-billed platypuses don't have stomachs, but they do have a digestive system that works without it.

Duck-billed platypuses can hold as many as 600 worms in their cheeks in one go.

When English scientists were given the first duck-billed platypus specimen brought back by explorers, they thought it looked so strange that they didn't believe it was a real creature and thought someone was playing a joke on them.

Rabbits

It's illegal to have a pet rabbit in the Australian state of Queensland, unless you can prove that you're a magician and that the rabbit is part of your show.

Baby rabbits have no scent at all, which helps keep them safe from predators.

In 1807, the French emperor Napoleon was scared away by rabbits. As a celebration, he had organised a rabbit hunt, but when they were released from their cages, thousands of the rabbits all charged towards Napoleon and he turned and ran away.

Rats

In 2008, scientists discovered that 4 million years ago, there were rats in South America that were the size of hippos and weighed one tonne. They nicknamed one fossilised specimen 'Mighty Mouse'.

Rats can fall over 15 metres and survive.

Rats are PEEING ALL THE TIME, wherever they go. They pee to impress females, they pee on each other – they even pee on the food that they want to eat!

Rats' teeth never stop growing throughout their life, but they keep them worn down by constantly chewing things. If they stopped chewing, their teeth would grow right through the tops of their mouths.

Reindeer

Reindeers' eyes change with the seasons – in the summer they have golden irises, but in winter they change to blue to help them see in the dimmer light.

From around 1899 in the USA, reindeer were used to deliver post in Alaska. The US Postal Service used the animals to cover distances of 30 to 50 miles, with each reindeer able to carry up to 140 kg of letters and parcels.

Rudolph the Red-nosed Reindeer is female, as are all the other reindeer that

pull the sleigh of Father Christmas. We know this because Rudolph and the others are always shown as having antlers. Male reindeer use their antlers to fight each other during the autumn breeding season, so by Christmas they have cast them off. Only females keep them through the winter period.

Rhinoceroses

14,000 years ago there were **woolly rhinoceroses** walking around. Their long, thick hair helped them to survive the extreme cold. We have found many mummified bodies of these huge animals frozen in the permafrost of northern Eurasia.

The African black rhinoceros is an astonishing pooper – it excretes its own weight in dung every 48 hours, which is an average of 682 kg a day.

Cacareco (who lived between 1954–1962) was a female **black rhinoceros** in Brazil. In 1958, during an election in the city of São Paulo, the citizens were so sick of their politicians that they decided to vote for Cacareco to run the city instead. She won 100,000 votes, more than any other politician in the competition. Sadly, even though she won, it was decided that you can't have a rhinoceros running a city, no matter how popular they are.

Seals, Sea Lions & Walruses

The Hawaiian name for the monk seal is *ilio holo i ka uaua*, which means 'dog running in rough seas'.

Sea lions love particular smells – not just fish, as you might assume, but they also go nuts for cinnamon, orange and banana. When scientists at the Institute for Marine Mammal Studies in Gulfport, Mississippi, USA, rubbed cinnamon on the walls of the sea lion enclosure to see what they'd do, one sea lion called Sage liked it so much that she started rubbing her body against the wall.

The Inuit people of Alaska use **walrus** whiskers as nose-picking tools. They also use walrus blubber (fat) to fuel their lamps, and can turn their guts into clothing, which the Inuit can eat if they need food.